You are

Vitamins
for the
Spirit

[signature]

Vitamins
for the
Spirit

Robert J. Danzig

Frederick Fell Publishers, Inc.
Hollywood, Florida

PUBLISHED BY

Frederick Fell Publishers, Inc. 2131 Hollywood Boulevard, Hollywood, FL 33020
1-800-771-3355   www.fellpub.com   E-MAIL: fellpub@aol.com

Danzig, Robert J., 1932-
Vitamins for the spirit / Robert J. Danzig.
p. cm.
ISBN 0-88391-000-4
1. Motivation (psychology) - Quotations, maxims, etc.
2. Achievement motivation - Quotations, maxims, etc.
3. Success - Psychological aspects - Quotations, maxims, etc. I. Title.
BF503.D36 1999
158.1'28 - dc21

98.31626
CIP

3 5 7 9 10 8 6 4 2

BOOK DESIGN BY Josh Klenert

ILLUSTRATION CREDITS ON PAGE 130

With great gratitude
for the privilege of guiding
Mary Elizabeth, Marsha Theresa,
Darcy Lynn, Steven Robert
and Matthew Brady
toward the unique
"Vitamins for the Spirit" they are.

Acknowledgment

For all who provided me a favorite combination of words that can serve to inspire — and — the lovely, rare in the universe pen and ink sketches of the gifted Hearst Newspapers artists, who share their abundant creativity — a Thank You.

Foreword

Preparing for a visit to my daughter, Darcy, in Dayton, Ohio — I had purchased a new personal organizer as a gift for her. While waiting for the accommodating sales lady to organize the organizer, my eye set on a display rack of cards with motivational quotes. Knowing that Darcy enjoyed motivational quotes, I purchased several. When I presented them to her, I observed that they were simply quotes on a card with no unifying theme.

Darcy thanked me and asked, "What unifying theme would you suggest were such cards produced by you?" My answer, after a moment's reflection, was to call them 'Vitamins for the Spirit.' Darcy responded that this was a 'big idea' and that I should go home and trademark it. I did.

When the trademark validation arrived, I decided to collect vitamins from mainly strangers who crossed my path over a 2-week period. Precisely 64 people came my way in 14 days — I asked that each send me a favorite motivational thought by e-mail or fax. Every single person did just that. I then sent each quote out to the art department of Hearst Newspapers and requested pen and ink sketches that reflected the artists' creative reaction to the motivating words. The result is this potpourri of lovely renderings which, combined with the motivating words are a source of inspiration to all who read and assimilate the pages.

Vitamins for the Spirit invites you to fill your day with inspiration.

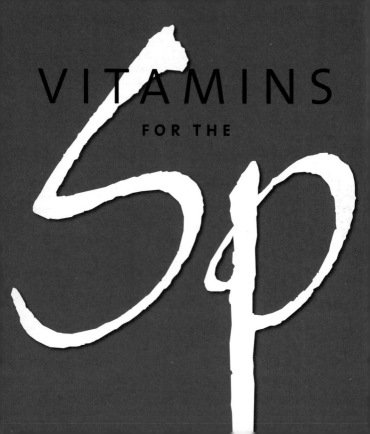

VITAMINS

FOR THE

The 10 most powerful two letter words:

IF IT IS TO BE

IT IS UP TO ME

ive words that stand between you and your dream:

I don't feel like it

*It is not **WHAT** you do for*

a living that is most

important — but —

***HOW WELL** you do it that*

makes the difference.

Hope that is seen is not hope,

for who hopes for what he sees?

But, if we hope for what we do not see,

we wait for it with patience.

Never Complain.

Never Explain.

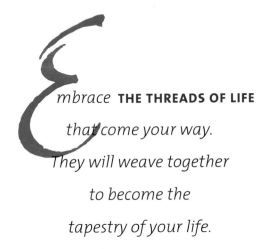

Embrace **THE THREADS OF LIFE**
that come your way.
They will weave together
to become the
tapestry of your life.

All glory comes

from daring to **BEGIN**.

Well done is

better than well **SAID**!

Many of life's failures are persons who did not realize how **CLOSE** *they were to* **SUCCESS** *when they gave up.*

The important thing in this world is not so much where we are — but — in what direction we are moving.

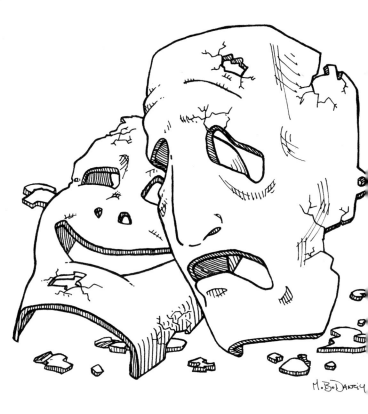

M. BoDANCiY

Do not wish to be

anything but what you are —

and try to be that

perfectly.

When you have done your

best—

You should wait for the result in

peace.

Holly Maltby

*Your **SPIRIT** — your will to*

excel and endure.

These qualities are much more

important than the events that occur.

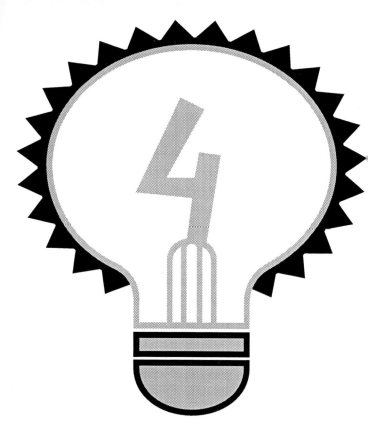

Four simple steps to accomplishment:

Plan purposefully

Prepare prayerfully

Proceed positively

Pursue persistently

We cannot direct the

winds–

but we can adjust the

sails.

Enthusiasm is the **PROPELLING FORCE** *for climbing the ladder of success.*

CHEER UP:

Birds have bills, too,

but they keep on

singing.

earn to pause...

Things worthwhile

can catch up to you.

Sally
QUINN-GRIMM

Life is in session.
Are you present?

Everyone
is
someone.

Justin Smith

Better to  at
doing **SOMETHING**

than to
succeed

at doing **NOTHING.**

Mark Joseph Sharer

How silent the woods
would be if only
the best birds sang.

Give me the **SERENITY**
to accept what **CANNOT** be changed,

the **COURAGE** to
influence what **CAN** be changed,

and the **WISDOM** to know
one from the other.

ever let yesterday

use up

too much of today.

hings turn out best
for those who make the best
out of the way
things turn out.

Think *a good day!*

Plan *a good day!*

Put good *into the day!*

A bell is no *bell*
until you ring it.

A song is no *song*
until you sing it.

Love isn't *love* until
you give it away.

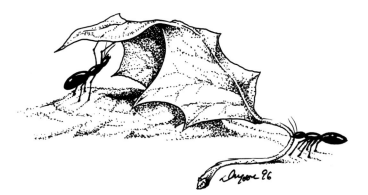

PRESS ON

*Nothing in the world
can take the place of persistence.*

*Talent will not;
nothing is more common than
unsuccessful men with talent.*

*Genius will not;
unrewarded genius is almost a proverb.*

*Education — alone — will not;
the world is full of educated derelicts.*

*Persistence and determination
alone are omnipotent.*

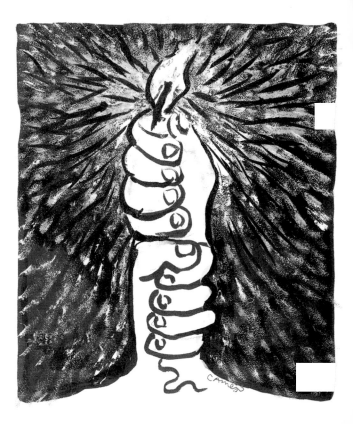

A CANDLE'S *but a simple thing, it starts with just a bit of string.*

*Dipped with patient hand,
it gathers wax upon the strand,
until complete and snowy white
it gives at last a lovely light.*

LIFE *seems so like that bit of string.*

*Each time we do a simple thing,
yet day by day on life's strand,
we work with patient heart and hand.*

*It gathers joy, makes dark days bright
and* **GIVES** *at last a lovely light.*

No life is so **HARD**
that one can't make it **EASIER**
by the way one **ACCEPTS** it.

Life by the mile is a trial.

Life by the yard is hard.

But — life by the

inch is a cinch!

*The will to win
is not nearly as important
as the will to*
PREPARE *to win.*

*Your mind is powerful enough to do more than one thing at one time, but you can only do one thing **WELL** at one time. Just do what you're doing while you're doing it.*

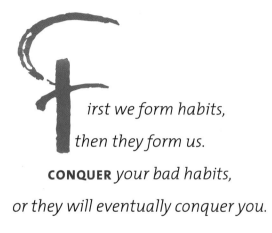

irst we form habits,

then they form us.

CONQUER *your bad habits,*

or they will eventually conquer you.

Do it!

Do it right!

Do it right now!

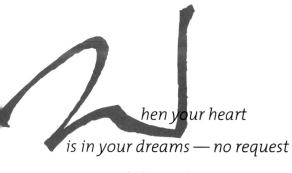

*hen your heart
is in your dreams — no request
is too extreme.*

*dversity causes some
people to break and others
to break records.*

*Life is like a grindstone, it either grinds
you down or it polishes you up.*

If better is possible,
good is not enough.

*Edison was asked how he dealt
with the 12,000 failures he experienced
in inventing the light bulb.*

*He said he never failed —
he just learned 12,000 ways **NOT**
to invent the light bulb.*

*What losers call failure
winners call **FEEDBACK**!*

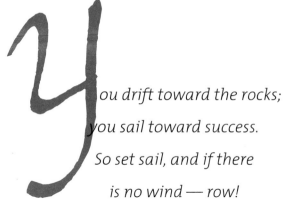

You drift toward the rocks;
you sail toward success.
So set sail, and if there
is no wind — row!

Be an action person.

Do not wait to get motivated

before you do something.

Do something and

then you will get motivated.

How to avoid criticism:

Say nothing

Do nothing

Be nothing

HOLLY MALTBY

If you do not

stretch

your limits, you will

SET *your limits.*

*Everything you need
is already inside you.
An acorn has everything
it needs to become an oak.*

A painter paints with his **HAND**.

An artist paints with his **MIND**.

But — a master *paints*

with his hand and his

mind through his **HEART**.

(RICHARD K. STODDARD)

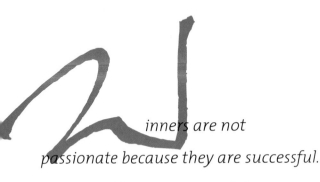

inners are not
passionate because they are successful.
They are successful
because they are passionate.

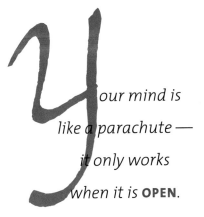

our mind is
like a parachute —
it only works
when it is **OPEN**.

People are like ten-speed bikes — most of us have gears we never use.

MONITOR YOUR SELF-TALK.

The words "can't," "if," "impossible,"

"maybe" and "try" are in the dictionary.

*But — they are **NOT** part of the*

*everyday vocabulary of **WINNERS**.*

5hoot for the moon.

Even if you miss,

you will be among the stars.

Do not coast. Nothing ever coasts **UPHILL**.

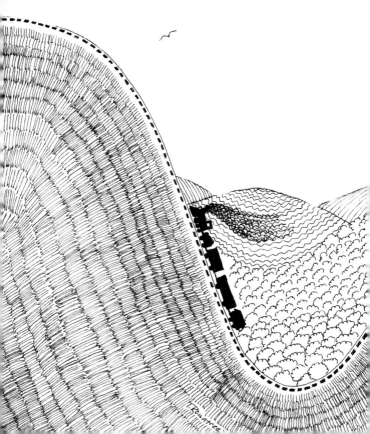

hether you think you **CAN** *or*
whether you think you **CAN'T** —
you are right in either case.

How much time you PUT IN is not as important as what you PUT INTO the time.

*ct the way you want to **BECOME** and you will become the way you **ACT**.*

You make a living *by what you* **GET**.

You make a life *by what you* **GIVE**.

5 keys to happiness:

Health

Love

Achievement

Expectation

Contrast

Ignite the leader within you. Polish up your:

Quality

Innovation

Inspiration

Perseverance

Passion & Enthusiasm

Character

Charisma & Energy

What a day
a
difference makes.

What you conceive in your mind and believe in your heart you will achieve.

If you do not know where you are going you might end up where you are heading.

A mistake is not failure — but feedback.

J.T. MENO

Winning does not lead to passion; passion leads to winning.

Love is invariably a two-way street —
a reciprocal phenomena
whereby the receiver also
gives and the giver also receives.

Inho 96

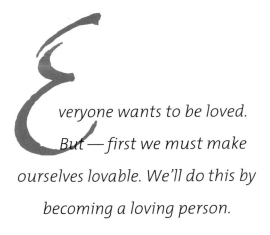

Everyone wants to be loved.
But — first we must make
ourselves lovable. We'll do this by
becoming a loving person.

(RICHARD K. STODDARD)

You have inner resources you never dreamed of.

You have hidden talents you have not used yet.

When you start tapping these powers, you will begin to do things you never thought you could do.

There is no limit to how great you can be.

The only limitations you have are the ones you set for yourself.

As you erase your limitations you will begin to tap more of your personal power.

It is all there for you to use.

The Illustrators

A special thanks to all of the wonderful
artists who donated their talents.

ARTIST	PAGE	AFFILIATION
Matthew B. Danzig	2	Wet Squirrel, Ltd.
Matthew B. Danzig	4	Wet Squirrel, Ltd.
Sally Quinn-Grimm	6	*Midland Daily News*
Dan de la Torre	8	*San Francisco Examiner*
Matthew B. Danzig	10	Wet Squirrel, Ltd.
Jill Feuk	12	*Houston Chronicle*
Matthew B. Danzig	14	Wet Squirrel, Ltd.
Doug Moore	16	Albany *Times Union*
Patrick Zeller	18	*San Antonio Express-News*
Matthew B. Danzig	20	Wet Squirrel, Ltd.
John T. Valles	22	*Midland Reporter-Telegram*
Holly Maltby	24	*Midland Daily News*
Joe Shoulak	26	*San Francisco Examiner*
Beena Mayekar	28	*Houston Chronicle*
Jeff Scheer	30	Albany *Times Union*
Matthew B. Danzig	32	Wet Squirrel, Ltd.
John T. Valles	34	*Midland Reporter-Telegram*
Sally Quinn-Grimm	36	*Midland Daily News*
Dan de la Torre	38	*San Fransisco Examiner*

ARTIST	PAGE	AFFILIATION
Justin Smith	40	*Houston Chronicle*
Mark Joseph Sharer	42	Albany *Times Union*
Patrick Zeller	44	*San Antonio Express-News*
Steve Greenberg	46	*Seattle Post-Intelligencer*
Judith Tate Meno	48	*Midland Daily News*
Dan de la Torre	50	*San Francisco Examiner*
Inho Kim	52	*Houston Chronicle*
Doug Moore	54	Albany *Times Union*
John Camejo	56	*San Antonio Express-News*
Ben Garrison	58	*Seattle Post-Intelligencer*
Sally Quinn-Grimm	60	*Midland Daily News*
Joe Shoulak	62	*San Francisco Examiner*
Beena Mayekar	64	*Houston Chronicle*
Rex Babin	66	Albany *Times Union*
Felipe Soto	68	*San Antonio Express-News*
John T. Valles	70	*Midland Reporter-Telegram*
Matthew B. Danzig	72	Wet Squirrel, Ltd.
Staff Artist	74	Hearst Newspapers
Jill Feuk	76	*Houston Chronicle*

ARTIST	PAGE	AFFILIATION
Greg Montgomery	78	Albany *Times Union*
John Camejo	80	*San Antonio Express-News*
Kim Carney	82	*Seattle Post-Intelligencer*
Holly Maltby	84	*Midland Daily News*
Joe Shoulak	86	*San Francisco Examiner*
Justin Smith	88	*Houston Chronicle*
Richard K. Stoddard	90	Albany *Times Union*
Felipe Soto	92	Albany *Times Union*
Cliff Vancura	94	*Seattle Post-Intelligencer*
Sally Quinn-Grimm	96	*Midland Daily News*
Gene McDavid	98	*Houston Chronicle*
Terry Rountree	102	*Houston Chronicle*
Doug Moore	104	Albany *Times Union*
James Hendricks	106	*San Antonio Express-News*
Duane Hoffman	108	*Seattle Post-Intelligencer*
Rebecca Agler	110	*Midland Daily News*
Matthew B. Danzig	112	Wet Squirrel, Ltd.
Terry Rountree	114	*Houston Chronicle*
Rex Babin	116	Albany *Times Union*

ARTIST	PAGE	AFFILIATION
Felipe Soto	118	*San Antonio Express-News*
John T. Valles	120	*Midland Reporter-Telegram*
Judith Tate Meno	122	*Midland Daily News*
Joe Shoulak	124	*San Francisco Examiner*
Inho Kim	126	*Houston Chronicle*
Richard K. Stoddard	128	Albany *Times Union*